Cottage Cats

Dedication

To all the cats in the world and the humans who love them.

Published by Sellers Publishing, Inc.

Copyright © 2009 Kim Jacobs
All rights reserved.

Edited by: Mark Chimsky-Lustig & Robin Haywood
Design: Heather Zschock
Production: Charlotte Smith

Sellers Publishing, Inc.
P.O. Box 818, Portland, Maine 04104
For ordering information:
(800) 625-3386 toll free
Visit our Web site: www.sellerspublishing.com • E-mail: rsp@rsvp.com

ISBN: 13: 978-1-4162-0538-8

10 9 8 7 6 5 4 3 2 1

Printed and bound in China.

Cottage Cats

My Companions on the Path to Joy

Kim Jacobs

SELLERS
PUBLISHING

where I want to be

My home is a cottage in Maine situated on a hill, surrounded by gardens. I look out over rolling hills patterned with fields and woods, covered by an ever-changing sweep of sky. Each season brings color and delight: the lilacs and lupine of spring, summer roses opening their blooms to the sun, a blaze of leaves in autumn, and the crabapple dropping its red fruit onto the bright snow, completing the year's full circle. This is my retreat, where I paint, write, and garden — and reflect on how to discover joy in everything around me. And if it eludes me elsewhere I know that I can always find it just by watching my cats play by the cottage door. This book is about all the cats who have been part of my life — through the calm times and the storms — and what they've taught me along the way.

a return to home

Life delivers lots of lessons, big and small, that often arrive unannounced. I've learned to appreciate these messages, although it hasn't always been easy.

Sometimes the lessons that I find most challenging turn out to be the ones I need most. At one time, I felt a deepening sense of despair — in which I questioned my own creativity and even my place in the world.

Everything changed when I discovered a lump in my breast. Facing cancer suddenly jolted me into an awareness of how vital every moment is. I had known this before, but hadn't fully realized it until then: that the best and worst of life requires living in the moment. This understanding helped me to feel a new sense of peace and happiness. Problems that had seemed so huge no longer mattered.

During this period, I found special comfort in my cat Malai. I believe she was truly sent to me for that short time. As if guided by something mysterious, Malai leapt onto me. It was then that I was first alerted to my condition. Returning weary from each medical leave, I always found her waiting by the door to welcome me home. When my mind, body, and spirit were strong again, she was gone . . . perhaps in search of someone else to comfort.

cool waters

My cats are my helpers, my muses. They sprawl across my papers as I sketch. My painter's eye watches them assume a perfect pose, but just as I'm about to capture the moment, in true cat fashion they leap away. On paper, I weave together what I see in front of me and what I see in my imagination to create something wholly new: my calico cat Baksheesh becomes Tiger Tom, leaning over the smooth stone coping of a fountain in Tuscany.

He laps the water that glints in the cool Mediterranean morning and his ginger stripes mirror the orange-flame curves of the trumpet flowers nearby.

~

My cats teach me to see the beauty in their nature. Their gift to me is their ability to just be.

connection

There once was a cat named Mrs. Smith who taught
me what it means to be a good human. I was
a little girl then, and Mrs. Smith was a stern
disciplinarian. One day she rode herd over my
little troop of friends, accepting no nonsense as
she escorted us across the field to the edge of the
lane. "Wait here," she seemed to be saying as she
looked both ways before allowing us to cross to
the other side. From her, I learned to care about
the needs of others, and not just my own. She
taught me to love and respect all the creatures
that I am lucky enough to share this world with.

priorities

Darn these weeds! I say to myself as I grab a handful, brushing aside the voluptuous pink peonies without a glance. I kneel, head down in the foliage, with Lucy weaving between my knees unnoticed. I'm attacking the pigweed that's become woven between the strappy leaves of the iris when suddenly Lucy pounces on it. "Lucy, you're not helping," I say but she continues sitting on every weed I intend to pull. I grab hold of witchgrass, which has rooted deep, and I tug it free from the earth with a swift yank. Poor Lucy who is hovering close, demanding attention, almost goes flying too. I call her to me and we lay together, my head on a pile of dandelions as Lucy purrs contentedly on my chest. I gaze up at the flowers and think, *Yes, Lucy, you're right. The weeds can wait!*

NINGSIDE COTTAGE

KimJacobs©

my muse

When the mail comes, it's Ooty's cue for his morning stroll through the garden up his favorite tree. His body is attuned to rhythms of the day. When I walk to my studio to paint, he follows to lend a helping paw. But he is soon in his favorite "yogic" position, paws folded inward, head resting against my knee and chanting his gentle purr. I sit, peacefully immersed in the divine sound.

contentment

You know how some people tape notes to their mirrors or refrigerators to remind themselves to "breathe, relax, and smile"? Or they turn over the pages of little calendars, which prompt them to "be alive!" and to "seize the day"? I don't need written reminders, I have my cats.

in harmony

After a long morning working in the garden, I hang up my wide-brimmed hat and find a cool spot inside to relax, but I am already thinking about what else I need to get done. My cats choose the sun and settle lazily into their garden chairs, as if they, too, have been pulling weeds all morning.

~

I remember Claudine, who was queen of the cat naps. She would sprawl in her half-sleep, eyes closed, but ears alert, totally at rest and yet ready for whatever came next. I imagine her on a stone bench in a fragrant garden. And later, as I paint her, I am transported there, too.

grateful for what I have

Surrounded by my gardens, fields, and woods, I live in a little paradise. I am thankful for it every day. If I lived in a more urban setting, surrounded by all the complexities of humans and human-made things, I would be doubly grateful for my cats. They are my little bit of nature packaged on four paws. They are my life's anchor, always honest, unpretentious, and true.

the gift of a smile

"Jeeeeerie! Where are you?" I call as I step outside to feel the sun on my face. Hearing a muffled meow, I see a tail snaking out from among the flower clippings that I gathered earlier in a basket. The cuttings rustle, the basket tips, rolls, and leaves cascade everywhere. Jeerie's little face appears hesitantly among the greenery. I smile. Lately, I've noticed that when I turn the corners of my mouth up in amusement, I feel a corresponding lift in my spirits. Scientists have even confirmed that the simple act of a smile makes all kinds of good things happen in your body. But today, how much better it is to smile spontaneously and feel such unexpected pleasure!

lucky to be here

Gobi and Dunia reach high on the rough wood of the gateway, their backs arching like perfect bows, as they pull their claws through the soft wood. It feels good, but they are also marking the gate with their scent, giving notice that this is their world. They come to me, in the part of the garden where I am busy pruning, and try to lend a helping paw or two. But first, they brush softly against my legs again and again. Surely, this feels good too, but I understand they are also marking me, giving notice that I am theirs. Here, in this wide world of the garden, woods, and fields — their natural element — they give me the honor of claiming me as their own.

cobblestone way

Like most creatures, cats like to play and today the game is hide and seek. Jeerie likes to play hard to get. I can see Ooty's frustration when he can't scout her out, even when he thinks he's on the trail. Then I wonder, perhaps Ooty knows where Jeerie really is and just wants to prolong the fun . . .

LAVENDER

CHIVES

COMFREY

witness

Timmer has his eyes fixed firmly on the cakes, as
if watching a mouse hole. I don't know what
he expects them to do. Jump up and run? He
doesn't twitch a muscle, except to make that
curious *ah-ah-ah-ah* sound of a cat on stakeout.
Such intention and focus on the task at hand
never ceases to amaze me.

I wait to see if he will pounce, but he restrains
himself. So I give him a little taste, but it doesn't
compare with his kibbles as cat fare and so he
nonchalantly walks away. I wish I could be so
casual when disappointments come my way!

Mushroom herb
Quiche

stillness

*Have you noticed the way cats can occupy a spot and
make it so much their own?* They are "there" with
such a sense of belonging. I think it has to do
with their complete and intense presence in any
given moment. Trina is happy as a clam on her
bicycle seat. She is "there" and nowhere else. She
is not already thinking about where she would
be happier, or where she had been happier in

Kim Jacobs ©

the past. I am starting to learn that for myself.
Caught up in the little cares of my life, I look to
Trina in all her "being there-ness" to help me find
my own "there" too.

inner light

I paint Chloe lazing in the sun and imagine her
and Lena in an exotic setting. She doesn't
drop names and casually mention the fabulous
little café she just loves on the Italian Riviera,
she simply climbs out of my arms to survey
her world from a perch on my shoulder, while
delivering satisfied purrs directly into my ear.
When she first came to us, she was a shy little
thing, avoiding my gaze and lying submissively
in my arms. Now, she insists on a place on my
shoulder and looks me in the eye with a distinct
air of superiority as if to say she is mistress of all
she surveys!

blissful

The cats wait impatiently for us to come to lunch, as
if to say, Don't you know where you should be?
And in a way, they're right — wherever they are
is home and it's a very good place to be.

water sports

Dori watches the door, eager for me to come out to the garden. She is fascinated by the sound of water sloshing in my watering can and she runs beside me as I make my rounds. She bats at the glittering droplets that fall and chases after the rivulets that snake through the primroses. As I pull the hose through the grass, she tracks its intriguing hiss and leaps up, surprised, each time it starts to slither by. Curiosity doesn't kill this cat — it makes her more alive!

contrasts

Fall's arrived and Boo is in a bad mood. She stares
Petey down. Earlier they had been viewing the
world happily together from the window, but
now Boo is determined to pick a fight. She
launches herself and they both fall with a thud,
their front legs wrapped around each other, their
back feet pummeling with Thumper-like rabbit
kicks. Petey escapes, is recaptured, and escapes
again. Then, as suddenly as it began, it is all over
and Boo is giving little licking kisses to Petey's
face. I wish my bad moods changed as quickly. If
everything depends on the state of mind we're
in, then I'm determined to find a bit of grace in
any situation. And with the help of my cats, I'm
getting closer to that all the time.

In the Gard

changing seasons

A pair of our cat companions came home with us in
November. After establishing their dominion
over every inside nook and cranny, they are now
ready to take on the great outdoors, where the
ground is covered in snow. After a few tentative
forays bring them bounding quickly back to the
cottage door, they begin to get the lay of the
land. And what a wonder it is to watch them,

two wild whirlwinds, a frenzy of black and
gray on white. They race the maze of shoveled

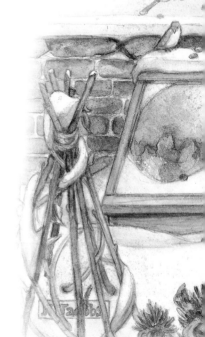

pathways, at times only the very tips of their
tails to be seen above the snow, like little flags
tracing their journeys of discovery.

sparkle

It's a joy of another flavor; the snow recedes and spring begins to gradually unfold as Ooty and Jeerie tumble over each other, so excited to check out everything. They zoom up trees with the rising sap and chase petals as they fall. They roll in the sprouting catmint and sample the greening grass. They mount ambushes in the jungle of multicolored tulips and finally stretch out with satiated smiles on the snow that melts into the sun-warmed earth.

dreams

So much to learn from our cat companions. They remind us of how we were before we tied ourselves round with worries, a time when we didn't need technological gadgets to stave off boredom, but knew how to find joy naturally in the simple things life presents to us all the time. So this spring, I follow the lead of my cottage cats, and contentedly watch the light dance through the delicate petals of the newly opened blossoms.

bounty

In summer, I watch my cats tear through the garden
with their sense of unfettered freedom. Gobi
rolls and wriggles languorously on her back,
between the broccoli plants, feet in the air. A
small dust cloud rises and settles over her fur,

and small bits of weeds poke out from behind
her ears. I call her my "dust ball cat" and she
jumps up on my lap, as if proud to answer to this
new name.

rosy promise

Today, the problems of the world have infiltrated my being. I can sense the black cloud looming and when that feeling approaches, I immediately begin a search for simple sources of wonder and delight. There's magic in this exploration. I find that with that first little intention of opening my eyes to the pleasure around me, a chain reaction begins. The more joy I feel, the more joy I find. Of course, the cats are a big part of the journey: they are the perfect catalysts (no pun intended) to set my transformation in motion.

wonder

I am shelling peas. We had a fine crop this year. The pods plunk into one bowl and the peas ping into another. Guinevere thinks it's great fun to fish over the rim with a dexterous paw, hooking one pod after another, and flipping them out onto the floor. Yawning, she stretches and places one paw over an errant pea. I reach down and trace the fine bones of her leg with one finger, touch the soft leather pads, one triangular and four perfect ovals, and stroke the silky fur. I am filled with wonder at the perfection of her body in all its awesome detail. Do we ever stop long enough to appreciate what's right in front of our eyes?

being attentive

I've been noticing Ooty's ears. He swivels them
forward and then back, tracking all the little
happenings that animate his world. Testing,
I make an odd noise. He brings them tautly
forward, keenly alert to the sound. That's what
I want for myself: to achieve that same intensity
of attention with which he honors everything.

catwalk

Aloo doesn't have to think about what she is going to wear today. She yawns, stretches, leaps from the bed, and she's off for the day. For her, there's no hunting through the closet for the right outfit or need to shop for clothes. She's ready for any activity no matter what kind of weather there is outdoors. And though I like to think that how I dress is just another creative outlet for me, I can't totally fool myself that there aren't some self-image issues involved. I do sometimes envy the honest simplicity and beauty of Aloo's natural attire.

stowaway

Toova is packed and ready to go. As I toss one last skirt towards my suitcase, I see the contents wiggle and shift. Lifting the top layers, I find Toova, tightly curled, shedding onto my clean sweaters and burrowing deeply into the once-neatly folded clothes. I like to think that she wants to travel with me, or perhaps she's trying to delay my departure. Or maybe, the suitcase has just proven to be an irresistible little bed . . .

She has been extra sweet lately, requesting more than the usual number of pick-ups, as if sensing I am going to be away for a long time. Being such an independent cat, her unexpected desire to tag along touches me. So here I am, missing her before I'm even gone.

KimJacobs©

sharing the bed

Seaport is our nocturnal wanderer. He finds our occupied bed an enticing terrain to be traversed. With a thump he arrives, and over hill and dale he goes, stopping to knead the slopes and perch momentarily on the highest spot, and then settles peacefully in the valley between us.

Aloo is the sound sleeper. She settles like a small mooring stone, pinning the sea of covers, creating a no-go zone for legs and feet. And we learn to confine ourselves to one small slice of bed, deferential even in sleep to this mistress of our affections.

all's fair

Every morning the rattle of doggy chow as it's poured into a dish brings Andy galumphing down the stairs. Pippy lies in wait and ambushes him from the curtain on the landing, batting at the flag of his tail with her paw. Down it goes to half-mast, but otherwise he pretends not to notice. Then with a leap, Pippy is over the rail, zooming like a racing car under Andy's belly to beat him to the bowl. Again, Andy pretends not to notice. But later, as he leaps onto the window seat for his mid-morning nap, he finds Pippy already there. Nonchalantly, he pins her to the cushion with one heavy paw and administers a long wet kiss with his very pink tongue. Pippy is off like a shot. That's all it takes for Andy to claim the window seat all to himself.

wild and tame

Armed with needle claws and sharp piercing teeth, my little Tiger Cat curls into my arms and purrs. I rest my cheek against her warm side with no fear. How amazing that this creature, who is capable of unleashing her fury like her wild cousins, instead trades her scratch for a soft paw, her bite for a lick, and her hiss for a purr, all for the sake of a bowl of milk, a warm hearth, and my human companionship.

claiming space

Chairs belong to cats. While I'm able to convince Arthur and Guinevere that a tabletop is off limits, I've had no such luck when it comes to chairs. They win, "paws down." There's no contest. They look at me as if to say, *You park yourself in a chair, why shouldn't we?* Whether they're lounging or surveying the scene, resting droopy-eyed or sprawling out on their backs, feet in the air, the armchair is the seat of choice.

learning

It's been a "one thing after another" day. All I want
is a soft chair, a book to disappear into and a
cat to settle quietly in my lap. But Sofia has
a different idea. She doesn't curl nicely into
a neat little package in the folds of my skirt,
but stretches along my leg, head blocking the
book propped on my knee. I shift to the other
knee. And so does Sofia. Awkwardly, I move
the book from right to left, right to left, like the
carriage of a typewriter, and try to scan the lines
bracketed between Sofia's two pointy ears. I
put the book down. I stroke her from the tip of
her nose to the tip of her tail and with her purr
comes my contentment. I don't need to escape
elsewhere. I can find what I want right here, if
I only just look.

joyful abandon

It's amazing how cats can turn anything into a
source of fun when they're in the mood to play:
a stray thread or piece of yarn or ribbon, a bit
of old leaf, even an eraser. Their joyful abandon
reminds me not to take myself so seriously, and to
look with fresh eyes at every object around me.

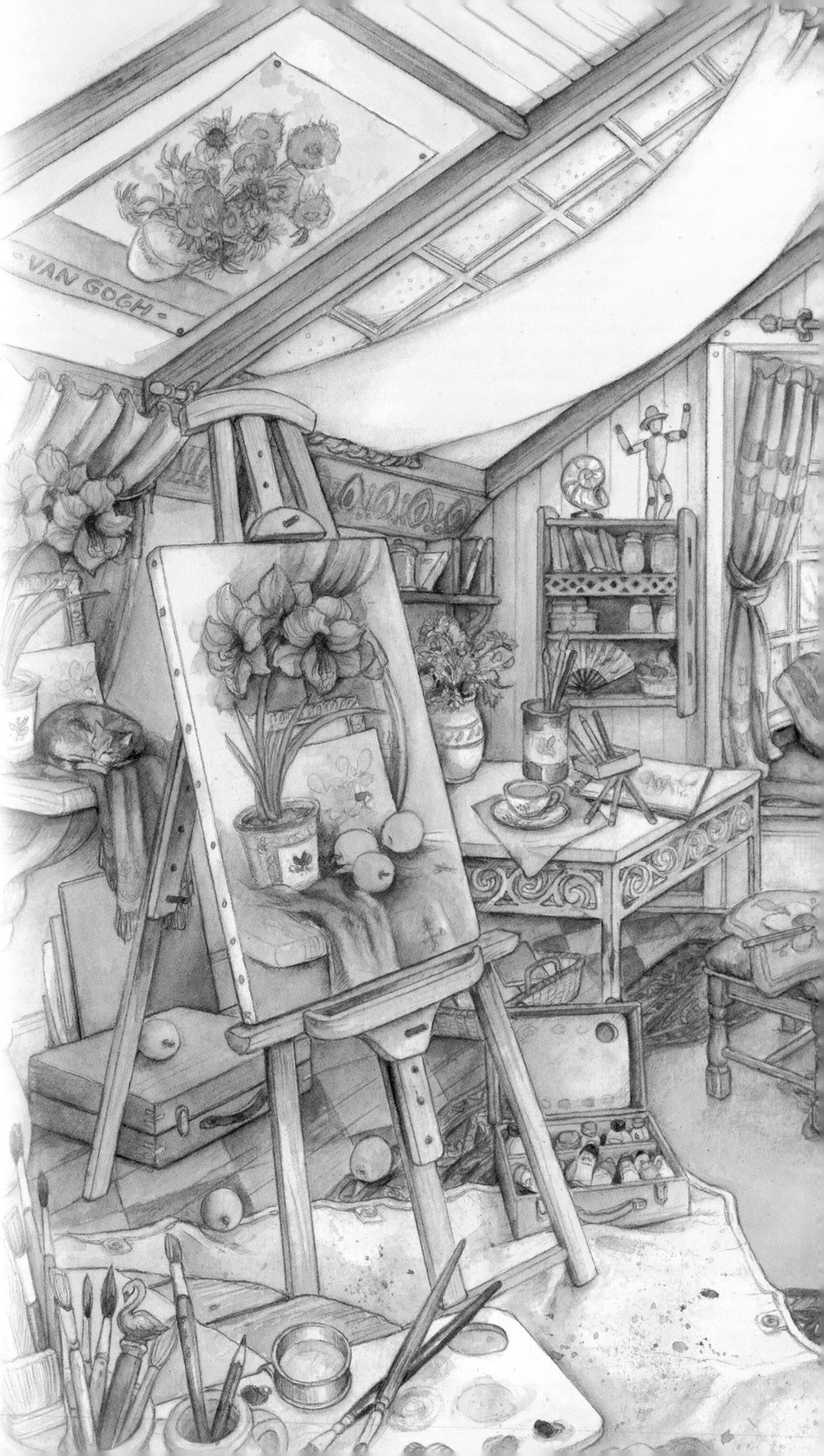
VAN GOGH

dawn

Ooty is the Cat-Who-Won't-Be-Held. He demands
attention in his own time and way, choosing
the most ungodly hour of the morning for his
petting session. He burrows under my blankets,
nuzzling his small noggin under my palm to alert
me that it's time for his favorite stroke, one long
glide from head to tail. He purrs like a dynamo
ten times his size. In a moment of blessed
silence, I feel his weight settle on my pillow and
then one small lick on the very tip of my nose.

seizing the moment

I receive my second kiss of the morning; this time, a flick of a rough tongue on my cheek from Gobi as I bend to place her bowl at her feet. How wonderful to be on the receiving end of her affection! Later in the day, as I sit with her in the garden room I think about that moment and the importance of letting those in our lives know how much we care about them. I suddenly recall the last time my sister visited me. As she was about to go through the security check at the airport, she turned to wave goodbye; I wanted to run to her and give her a kiss, but I hesitated, feeling awkward. Next time I won't let such an opportunity slip by . . .

inspiration

Tiger Cat helps me to write at my computer. She dangles a languid paw over the edge of the desk and, revealing her vast experience with "mice," she hooks the tail of my mouse with one sharp claw and swings it across the pad. When I recapture it, she turns her sights elsewhere, tipping my pencil cup, and scattering the pens and pencils everywhere. Then she's off like a shot, batting them across the desk, then the floor, flipping them high in the air. Every line of her body expresses her pleasure. If only I could be as eloquent with the lines I write and draw! Grabbing my pad, I scribble words and I sketch furiously, inspired to create another offering for these pages, hoping to capture some of the joy my cats have brought me.

on the path

And now Ooty has run off with my pencil. Maybe he's trying to tell me something — perhaps it's time to stop drawing and writing about "being there" and to just get on with it and live. In the end, perhaps that's what all my cottage cats have tried to teach me, each in their own way: that the path to joy is about experiencing the delight of every moment. By worrying less about the past and what's to come, we can become more of who we are.

acknowledgments

I want to express my gratitude

~ for the teachings of Eckhart Tolle;

~ for the help of the team at Sellers Publishing
in presenting my art so beautifully and for
making the musings of a painter resemble,
somewhat, the writings of an author;

~ for the patience of my big Leo, husband Bob;

~ and for all my cat companions through the years.